10 X GIVING

NON-PROFITS BASED ON 10 X THINKING

Copyright © 2021 by Dane E. Rose

dane@happinessdata.org

www.10XLiving.org

CONTENTS

- The 10 X Paradigm ………………………………………… 5
- What is Intelligence? ………………………………………… 7
- A 10 X Non-Profit ………………………………………… 9
- Sustainable Human Well-Being ……………………………… 11
- The Quest ………………………………………………….. 13
- Leverage ………………………………………………….. 15
- Transcending Culture ……………………………………….. 17
- Four Brains and their Operating Systems …………………… 21
- Reducing Trauma …………………………………………… 33
- The Most Significant Equation ……………………………… 35
- Changing Memes for Pennies ……………………………… 43
- The Most Valuable Database ………………………………... 51
- Template for a 10 X Non Profit …………………………… 55
- 10 X Idea ………………………………………………….. 61
- Pathways to Reality ………………………………………… 69
- Directions to Aim For ……………………………………… 71
- $1 Billion Spent Intelligently ……………………………… 77
- About the Author …………………………………………… 89

THE 10 X PARADIGM

Imagine you are bicycling to work and realize that your commute is taking up two hours a day, exposing your life to reckless drivers and your lungs to city smog. You want to be more efficient and set a goal of taking 10% less time to get to work each day. What would you do?

If you are like most people, you will peddle 10% faster and arrive at work, a little short of breath, 10% sooner as a result. This is because we can almost always improve an existing protocol 10-30% by just doing it faster. Because small, incremental improvements to any system are possible and simpler than designing a whole new system, we don't shake up our ideas with a goal to get 10-30% better results. If we set out to improve our results by 1000% we are forced to examine the entire paradigm and protocol with fresh eyes. In the case of getting to work, this may mean switching to ride hailing or deciding to work from home several times a week, eliminating the commute altogether. In the case of sending letters, we did not grant post office employees the exclusive right to drive faster than the speed limit. Instead, we invented email and saw communication arriving 1000 times faster and cheaper than letters.

Having a 10 X goal is the equivalent of asking ourselves and everyone involved to re-design everything from scratch, with the possibility of a cheaper, faster, more effective outcome by using new systems, such as e-mail. If we had simply asked postal workers to deliver mail 10% faster, we would never have conceived of an idea such as e-mail and would be paying 1000 times more for slower communication.

In beginning with the question: "How can our giving be 10 times more effective than the status quo?" we are exploring designs that are outside our current norms.

WHAT IS INTELLIGENCE?

Human intelligence can be measured by the efficiency with which an individual or organization transforms energy (time, money, and natural resources) into sustainable well-being for themselves and others.

Every human in the history of the species has innately desired to feel better and avoid feeling worse. Our intelligence determines how successful we are with that goal. A person, or organization, with low intelligence consumes vast amounts of time, money, and natural resources and generates high levels of chronic suffering for themselves and others. A highly intelligent individual or group takes very little time, money, and natural resources to generate results that vastly improve their own and others' sustainable well-being.

The intelligence of a culture can be measured by the conversion rate of a unit of time, money, and natural resources into units of sustainable well-being.

A 10 X NON-PROFIT

All human enterprise is directly related to the goal of increasing human well-being. A company, in a capitalist framework, has as its goal: making money for the owners and employees of the company. Money is a medium of exchange, the purpose of which is to increase the well-being of those who use it by exchanging something we value less for something we value more.

In order for a company to make money it must provide the perception of value to its customer. A customer will generally spend their money in response to the question: "What purchase or investment will bring me the most well-being now, or in the future?" In situations filled with pain and fear, the focus will be more short-term in nature (what can I do to stop this pain now!) and in peaceful and abundant situations the focus will be on investing in the future.

A non-profit, as with every other enterprise, aims to increase human well-being. However, it can afford to do so in ways that few individuals would prioritize for their next purchase by being more long term. For example, planting trees is highly intelligent for the species over the next 1000 years. However, few people worried about rent, credit card debt, or fixing their car will spend limited funds paying someone to plant trees for their children and grand-children's future well-being.

A 10 X non-profit is an enterprise directly aiming to generate as much sustainable human well-being as possible with a given amount of energy (time, money, and natural resources). When it generates 1000% more sustainable human well-being per unit of energy invested than the norm it is being compared to, it is a 10 X Non-Profit. As such it can be the most successful and profitable enterprise on the planet, benefitting from the compounding impact of long periods of time with no need for an immediate profit. To assess this we must use many of the measuring protocols of the best for-profit companies to ensure that every unit of energy is getting a high yield in well-being over time.

SUSTAINABLE HUMAN WELL-BEING

Cocaine, chocolate cake, and social media likes can create an expedient dopamine rush for a short time. However, consuming more and more sugar or other drugs is not sustainable, often resulting in a crash. Much like consuming credit-card debt to buy luxury nick-knacks, or an affair that destroys the trust in a quality relationship, the immediate short-term gratification is followed by a long reduction in mental, emotional, and physical well-being.

Sustainable human well-being results from a pattern of thinking, feeling, speaking, doing, and being that invests in resources that provide more and more well-being over time. Think of building the organic matter in soil to grow an organic garden, or installing solar panels that reduce our dependency on the grid and our utility bills. To determine how sustainable a path to well-being is, we have to measure well-being, as well as understand where the path is leading. For example, planting a tree suitable for a given location predictably leads to cleaner air for human lungs, as well as a reduction of temperature volatility, an increase in shade, erosion control, and may provide aesthetic beauty or some kind of food. A redwood will do this for 1000 years. A pine tree for 150 years. An apple tree for fifty years. If we understand the patterns we are in relationship with, we can measure the amount of well-being created over time with a given action.

Our well-being is expressed in mental, emotional, and physical dimensions, each of which is equally important. We each depend on our ecology and our physical health for our well-being. Being in great shape in a city filled with smog is as damaging to our well-being as being in terrible shape in a country with clean air.

Measuring well-being successfully on multi-dimensions is an art form I explore this in-depth in a series of videos at: https://10xwellbeing.com

THE QUEST

Every question is a quest that leads the quester on a journey into the unknown. A great question points in the direction of an area of the unknown that when explored, yields sustainably high levels of well-being.

The question I invite you to explore is this:

What is the single most intelligent thing that you are capable of doing to create the highest amount of sustainable well-being for the most people (including yourself) with the least amount of time, money, and natural resources? If you set out to design the most intelligent project for global well-being in the history of Earth, what would you do, and why would you do it?

In subsequent chapters, we will break this quest into smaller steps. Here are a few windows into the territory:

- What skill were you to learn it expertly, could provide the most value to the species over the next 100 years?
- Where does your culture create the highest levels of chronic suffering in its population?
- What problems, if unsolved, represent the biggest threat to humanity?
- If you were tasked with spending $1 billion with the goal of creating the most sustainable well-being for the most people over the next 1000 years, how would you spend it?
- What technology, if invented, could decrease the suffering on the planet by 1000%?

Now, what are ten steps you could take to move closer to an effective response to this quest?

What are the two most potent of the ten answers to this question?

Will you do them?

LEVERAGE

Archimedes once said: "Give me a long enough pole and a strong enough fulcrum upon which to push, and I could move the earth." Leverage is the process of amplifying our impact so that the same amount of energy creates bigger results. Here are some examples of leverage:

- Earning compound interest on an investment turns a little bit of money into a lot of money with time.
- Time turns a few drops of water a minute in a cave into a stalagmite after thousands of years.
- Recommending a book to one person that radically changes their life leverages ten minutes of our time with an existing book to have far more impact than we could have without that book.
- Recommending a book to one camera that projects an image to many people and changes ten thousand years leverages ten minutes of our time to have ten thousand times more impact than speaking to one person.
- Planting redwood trees today that will continue to grow for one thousand years, each sequestering over 1,500 tons of CO_2 from the atmosphere, is leveraging life's patterns to clean the air long after we are dead.

Any time we partner with an existing pattern of energy in a way that amplifies our results, we are using leverage. The more leverage we utilize, the more efficient we become. The more efficient we become, the more capacity we have to generate higher levels of well-being while consuming less energy in the process. In other words, leverage = intelligence, when that leverage creates sustainable human well-being.

The intelligent person asks themselves how they can have the most positive impact over time with the least amount of effort. The answer is partnering with as many existing technologies as possible that conserve their energy while amplifying results. Most of us use leverage all the time:

- I'm using words to describe ideas rather than showing you the ideas in action in person, saving 99% of both our energy in the process.
- I'm writing the words, rather than speaking the words in person, saving another 99% of energy that would be needed to get our bodies in the same place.
- I'm writing this once in a book that will be printed more than one hundred times, saving another 99% of my time and energy.
- I'm using the post office rather than delivering the book around the world in person, saving another 99% of time and energy.

In subsequent chapters, the theme of leverage will recur many times in different ways, because leverage is key to optimizing intelligence.

TRANSCENDING CULTURE

Culture equates to massive leverage by influencing 90% of our daily behavior and turning it into an unquestioned routine. Since our daily routines affect our lives and experience of life more than anything else, updating a cultural norm into a new best-practice can save millions of lives and massively increase well-being.

Anthropologists estimate that 10,000 cultures have existed in human history, each with its own language, belief system, and memes. 95% of those cultures are dead and more cultures and languages die every year as the last person to speak that language dies. In less than a million years everything we do, say, and think and the language we use will become so irrelevant to the reality of the future that it will no longer exist and seem far more backwards than life only a thousand years ago through our eyes.

The root word in culture is "cult." A cult is a self-referential pattern of thinking, feeling, speaking, doing and being:

- We do X because everyone in our cult is doing X and we want to fit in.
- Everyone today is doing X because their parents did X.
- Their parents did X because their parents did X.

Rather than looking outward, being flexible, intelligent and responsive to new data, cults define themselves by the unquestioned past. Cults that become extinct fail to adapt to a changing world and successfully enable their people to fulfill their human needs:

1. To survive.

2. To be secure in that survival.
3. To experience love and belonging.
4. To have high levels of self-esteem.
5. To develop personal talents.
6. To bring value to self and others with those talents abundantly.
7. To be part of something greater than self.

Every culture has "dead wood" in it: areas of tradition that actively impede the direct creation and maintenance of efficient levels of well-being. In these areas a culture weakens its people, making them vulnerable to death or absorption by a more intelligent cultural identity.

A culture is an identity: A habit of thinking, feeling, speaking, doing, and being. This identity pattern yields a statistical level of human well-being. A highly intelligent culture consumes relatively low amounts of time, money, and natural resources while ensuring that everyone who adopts the culture has 99% odds of fulfilling all seven basic human needs. Every cult in human history has told its children: "Our way is best. Our way is the only way. Copy us and you will survive. Deviate from the pact and you will not survive." When a generation believes this statement without re-thinking it, a certain percentage of people in that generation will lead miserable lives or die.

To transcend cultism in culture one must make a fundamental choice:

- Do I want to be normal and fit in, no matter the cost?
- Do I want to be exceptionally successful, happy, creative, innovative, and in an intelligent relationship with my underlying ecology?

Choosing happiness (the fulfillment of needs) over normalcy (the automatic acceptance of cultural norms) is a foundational decision that must be made as an individual or group before the changes are probable out of which 10 X results emerge. Our personal identity is a micro-culture: "I do, say, think, feel and be this way because this is the way that I have been thinking, feeling, speaking, doing and being for some time. I resist change because "that's not me," without evaluating the importance of the change to my well-being."

FOUR BRAINS AND THEIR OPERATING SYSTEMS

Our personal identity, initially downloaded from our culture, defines more than 90% of our daily thoughts, feelings, words, actions, and ways of being. It is colored and influenced by the region of the brain we are operating from and its default protocol. Given that human behavior has more impact on the planet's survival or destruction than any other species on earth, learning how to change that behavior in a direction conducive to sustainable life by updating our personal and cultural operating systems is a tool with massive leverage. Let's explore each brain's operating system and how it affects our lives.

The reptilian brain inside the brain-stem of every human uses a 200-million-year-old alligator operating system. The operating system references the law of mass and has a ruthless and simple protocol: Fight and consume the resources of smaller and weaker energy patterns. Run and hide from larger and stronger energy patterns. Freeze when neither of those options is available. Through this competition to survive, life breeds brains and bodies that became more and more competent at fulfilling the most basic need to survive.

Life's operating system among early animals can be summed up as:

- Divide and create vast quantities of energy patterns.
- Iterate and mutate to increase variety.
- See which patterns live and which ones die out.
- Ensure that the most competent and intelligent life forms consume the least competent and unintelligent life forms, thus systematically generating higher and higher levels of competency on the planet.

The reptilian operating system constantly kills off weakness, stupidity, incompetency, and waste, feeding these to the most efficient and well-designed patterns of energy in the ecology, in an up-cycling process. One way to imagine this would be a game of 3D printing in which life prints a million different designs randomly, lets them engage with one another, and prints more of any design that holds its structural integrity, while it recycles the raw material of any design that collapses or cannot sustain itself. Life does this until all of its designs are so efficient that they are ready to evolve into something even more intelligent.

On top of the reptilian brain, the rational brain emerges with an additional operating system:

- Observe sensory data.
- Replay sensory data through memory, looking for patterns.
- Discern and test our perception of patterns by seeing how well they allow us to predict the future.
- Develop models of reality through language that help us simplify overwhelming complexity.
- Continue to refine and develop our ability to predict the future and make choices, based on those predictions, that increase our ability to survive so successfully that we become secure in that survival.

The combination of the reptilian brain and the rational brain creates a synergy that is still unfolding today, resulting in increasing efficiency of transforming energy into the fulfillment of our survival and security needs. By combining the reptilian brain with the rational brain, we have become the most efficient pattern of energy on earth at generating never before seen products and services, ideas, beliefs, and ways of living. By being able to analyze data and iterate a protocol to more and more efficient heights we see a 1,000-fold increase in efficiency, relative to a humanoid body without the ability to speak, use language, do mathematics, and remember patterns of energy over time.

One could say that the purpose of the reptilian operating system is to compete for the right to survive on the basis of strength, or, to reference human warfare: "might is right." One could say that the purpose of the rational brain is to transfer the odds of survival to those who most successfully observe, analyze, and utilize that analysis to create massive amounts of efficient productivity, otherwise known as "security." Today, harnessing the technology of computers, it is a group of coders and inventors of the synthetic rational brain that are influencing and gathering resources more than any other group.

One can be the most brilliant, wealthy, and powerful reptile on the planet with the brain and technology to compete successfully for resources in a competition with billions of people and have no joy, empathy, warmth, or care for others. Capitalism rewards the rational reptile above all else with money, rank, and power, but it cannot generate a single friend. This is the function of the empathic brain and operating system, allowing us to transcend the human animal and become a human being able and willing to give and receive a sense of love and belonging, which is the third in our hierarchy of human needs.

The empathic brain is the opposite of the reptilian brain. When a company like Microsoft sees a new, better product on the market, it will seek to destroy or consume that company, so as to protect its monopoly and stop clients from having a viable alternative, while the empathic operating system is the antithesis of this: From a position of strength, the larger pattern of energy protects and cares for the smaller pattern of energy, generating trust and gratitude in a trustworthy relationship based on synergy over competition.

The diversion from reptilian protocols is seen in the asking of two questions: The reptilian brain looks for low-hanging fruit for exploitation: "Who is the weakest, most vulnerable, most gullible and naive person in our midst with energy that I can take, steal, manipulate and use for my purposes?" In a battle, the reptilian brain assesses the area in the enemy where they can cause the most pain and proceeds to cause that pain systematically for the purpose of extermination, revenge, or conquering resources. The empathic brain also starts with the question: "Who is in the most pain? Who is most vulnerable? Who has the most need right now?" However, for the empath, the purpose of understanding this is in order to ask and answer the second question: "How can we help reduce that pain and facilitate well-being?"

In summary:

- The reptile seeks to understand the vulnerabilities of others so that they can be used and exploited for personal, corporate, or national gain.
- The human being, differentiated from the reptile by empathy, seeks to understand the most vulnerable pain-point in their ally in an abundance paradigm so that they can help minimize that pain and, in the process, create a trustworthy relationship in a trust-based operating system.

Responding to pain with healing is built into the operating system of empathy, based on a belief in abundance, and on awareness that through empathy, your pain feels like my pain and so I will treat it as if it is my own. Empathy bridges the gap between the isolated identity of the individual and the larger identity of the relationship, or group. When we own the group and will not betray the group for personal gain we are in the territory of the empathic brain and operating system, and all of the abundance that cooperative synergy unlocks.

As a culture, we are roughly 70% rational reptile and 30% rational empath, reflected in behavior statistics that are mostly fear-based and pivot towards love-based when we feel safe enough with specific people in specific circumstances. As such we have not realized the more than 90% increase in efficiency and well-being that correlates with a 100% empathic operating system between human beings.

It is the pivot from rational reptile to rational empath that presents so many challenges for us today. The biggest challenge is that the more empathic we are, the more painful it is to encounter a human animal operating with the rational-reptile operating system. That pain is hard to stomach, so we often retreat into the anesthetized regions of our rational reptilian brain to navigate these relationships. While in that state, we hurt others who are in an empathic state towards us.

We can think of the fragility of the empathic operating system when we imagine the following image: One hundred Buddhist monks sit in a circle chanting "peace to the world" and feeling empathic. Then one person enters the temple with a gun using the rational reptilian operating system to figure that monks would be easy to attack and there should be gold in the temple. After killing one monk to instill fear, and taking another monk hostage, they then proceed to take the gold-plated statues from the altar and drive off. Hearing of this successful theft, other rational reptiles repeat the protocol in temples around the country until the military is called in to guard the temples, and several criminals are executed.

What can we learn from this picture?

- The first thing we see is that the sociopathic behavior of one person brought grief, sadness, rage, and trauma to one hundred monks, who must do a lot of work before they can sincerely go back to chanting from a place of goodwill.

- The second thing is that the rational reptile is kept in check by fear of harm, requiring a military response with equally sociopathic behavior in the form of executing the criminals.
- The third thing is that the transition into 100% utilization of the empathic brain and its operating system requires effectively healing the trauma of every individual, not just a select few. For a thief to kill a monk for gold, their own empathic brain must be almost completely numb. No one gets that way and stays that way through childhood, adolescence, and grown-up years without massive sociopathic protocols in parenting, education, and general culture, along with a decision to "mind our own business" and avoid people who are clearly in a lot of need. Sociopathic behavior feeds the reptilian brain, resulting in more sociopathic behavior, which reflects back at the world. This is why to move fully into empathy as an operating system we will need to prioritize the most traumatized, lonely, and unhappy people in the world as a species since it only takes one country to start a world war.

Just as the rational reptile is 1000 times more successful than the irrational reptile at generating security and abundance, so the movement towards a fully empathic operating system is 1000 times more efficient and effective at increasing sustainable human well-being than the rational reptile. It will take an enormous amount of effort to facilitate the pivot from rational reptile to empathic human being as the dominant operating system, so it's worth looking at why this pivot is as incredibly valuable for us as a species:

- All action taken from the rational reptile is fear-based: "I will lock the door because I don't want someone to steal my things. I will supervise my employees so they won't steal or be lazy. I will fence my farm so my animals don't escape. I will invest in nuclear weapons so others won't attack me and I can attack them. I will buy insurance in case things go wrong. It's not fun to do everything out of fear all of the time. Being a totalitarian dictator is not fun either.

- All action taken out of empathy is love-based: "I will cook for this person who would enjoy my food. I will make this product to help someone. I will write this book to be useful. I will offer this suggestion because I think good things will come of it." It is much more enjoyable to live in a state of empathic love with other empathic and loving people than it is to live in a state of fear with other fearful and sociopathic people.
- In order to survive and be secure in a reptilian operating system we must wage two wars simultaneously:
  - The first war is competing with everyone else for scarce money, time, and natural resources to survive and feel secure in our survival.
  - The second is taking steps to ensure that others will not take what we have secured for ourselves by erecting fear-based deterrents.

Let's look at both of these things in more detail. Competing in a paradigm of scarcity is vastly more difficult than collaborating to fulfill our human needs. Think about office politics: Someone, who knows exactly how you are about to fail, withholds the information you need so that they get your job while undermining the company's profits and shareholder wealth, and by doing so, the entire economy. Aside from the misery of living in a world of smiling faces who back-stab us, and the toll this takes on our heart, mind, and body, it's incredibly wasteful. Contrast that with everyone rooting for everyone to win in an abundance paradigm in which there are more and more opportunities for people to play the roles they wish to play virtually and physically and the level of waste goes down significantly. Now let's look at all the time, money, worry, effort, and natural resources we spend to stop others from behaving sociopathically towards us:

- Police infrastructure: Imagine all people in the police force, all people training police officers, all police cars, and all police buildings repurposed with the goal of minimizing global human suffering.
- Imagine all attorneys, judges, court-rooms, prisons, prison guards, caterers for prisoners, builders of barbed wire fences planting trees and creating public gardens.
- Imagine all global military budgets to the tune of trillions of dollars ensuring that everyone in every country has a safe warm bed to sleep in and nourishing healthy food.
- Imagine school systems repurposed so that teachers could learn an art or skill that helps local well-being and the children that like them as people and enjoy that skill can apprentice at a young age for free, rapidly gaining a level where they are net-contributors.
- Imagine most office buildings re-purposed for ecological adventures or theater as people are trusted to do what they love and are good at doing while at home, rather than leaving their homes empty and creating massive amounts of traffic.
- Imagine all global alarm companies shutting down so their employees could learn to grow organic food, bake, and give great massages.
- Imagine the generosity and gratitude you would feel, knowing that everyone in your neighborhood had your back and that you could depend on everyone to follow best-practices out of shared empathy in any situation?
- Imagine the increased health and well-being if all doctors and medicine, as well as the regulators, would focus on the long-term well-being of each person cared for, starting with a priority on prevention?
- Imagine if everyone involved in scams and fraud spent that time solving complex problems such as nuclear fusion and new forms of cheap power?
- Imagine if all the immigration protocols around the planet were designed for shared well-being so that all walls, check-points, and security could be re-purposed to make each place more enjoyable to live in?

75% of human time, money, and natural resources would naturally be re-directed towards 10 X well-being projects if fear-based concerns were eliminated by co-creating an informed, trustworthy species at a global level. To go from fearing for your child's safety to being excited about what they will learn about themselves is such a massive leap in well-being it is hard to grasp at this stage. However, it is life's next operating system and we are on an unavoidable path towards realizing its full potential with a possible detour into another world-war or two along the way to highlight the huge costs of remaining complacent in a rationally reptilian state.

It may be too much to hope to see anything this intelligent on a global level in our lifetime because it requires the willing participation of everyone to succeed. However, little is preventing this from happening in small, self-contained groups of fifty to one hundred people who have enough competency and empathy to light the way for humanity. www.MedicinaCR.org is one such community that you are welcome to explore with me.

The transcendent brain and its operating system: We currently utilize our transcendent brain in certain Near-Death Experiences, some orgasms, certain psychedelic sessions, breath work, and extreme physical endurance rituals. Through both traumatic and ecstatic dissociation from our body, we wake up to a part of us that has never been separate from any part of reality and feel deep love from and for All That Is. We don't need to spend much time exploring this operating system, which will be born organically in the abundant love of a world created out of empathy.

Transcendence is our doorway to divine connection: the consciousness that links all things as part of the greatest synergy in existence: life, the Universe, and Everything! Transcendence is also our path to the highest state of grace/efficiency and excellence. Once we identify as the whole, rather than a specific human body, we will have a better sense of how our body can best synergize with the whole in life, death, creativity, and change. To utilize the full human capacity without conflict, egos battling with other egos and informed with direct real-time data offers the chance for constant ecstatic growth, creativity, and life in an astonishing way that we can only glimpse.

As life has evolved from primordial slime into the human body with a reptilian brain, we can see a thousand fold increase in the complexity and efficiency of intelligence. This increases another 1000 times as the rational brain is added to the reptilian brain. As empathy is poised to become the next dominant operating system, in the form of the rational empath, within the next thousand years, we are poised with yet another thousand fold increase in the possibility field and in human well-being. This will be repeated as we move into the transcendent brain as the primary operating system at some point in our future.

The key question that defines the transcendent operating system is this: "How can I engage in a way that is best for the whole?" This makes no sense to ask as long as we feel separate from the whole in an either/or paradigm. It only takes hold naturally as we start becoming aware of our innate connection with all of life on every level. This takes skill and the time needed to create a far more rich and beautiful relationship with our world. It is leverage at work on the biggest scale.

The greatest human pain is the sense of being separate from self, others, the world, and God/Goddess, as well as being frightened of our projected versions of each of these. Moving into the transcendent areas of the brain, accessible in altered states, the fear of death, change, ourselves and the world reduces, while our adaptability, flexibility, and love increases.

Life knows what it's doing. If we are to pay tribute to the prevailing mythology of science, life gave birth to our universe some fifteen to twenty-five billion years ago, beginning with a mass of energy less than the size of a pea. If you are life, and you have created everything in existence from virtually nothing, that's a great track record! If you are life and you created billions of life forms on this planet alone, starting with algae, that's not a bad track record either. If you created a human being out of a reptile, that's not shabby work. In short, it seems likely that our transcendent brain is a massive step towards evolution.

What is important to understand is that in highly traumatic environments, with low levels of traumatic literacy and repair, the reptilian brain emerges in childhood as the predominant brain, reducing probable human beings to reptiles, with a sophisticated pattern-recognizing brain overlaid to create incredibly sophisticated human animals in a sociopathic state. The ecology and the brain are one: sociopathic cultures create traumatic experiences which stimulate the reptilian brain and the sociopathic operating system, which result in behavior that creates a sociopathic environment.

Highly empathic and intelligent cultures create an environment in which every human being has a 99% odds of fulfilling all their human needs as a community commitment. This creates a deep sense of fulfillment in which transcendent states naturally develop from time to time, leading to the evolution towards a safe and synergistic culture without violence.

One can lose one's humanity by being traumatized by a level of pain in which the empathic brain dissociates and shuts down to avoid feeling that pain. We can dehumanize a person by failing to become traumatically literate and helping them heal recurring trauma before it becomes PTSD. There is nothing more fundamental to intelligence, evolution, and life than whether we, as a culture, dehumanize the children born into it or facilitate their full potential as a transcendent human being. Any community that makes a commitment to fulfilling the needs of each of its members can create human beings out of animals and adults out of traumatized children in grown-up bodies.

REDUCING TRAUMA

The more perceived threats to an individual or national identity, the more trauma will be experienced individually and nationally. The more trauma is experienced, the more active the reptilian brain becomes. The more active the reptilian brain becomes, the more a human being regresses into a sociopathic state, otherwise known as a human animal. Using the fight/flight/freeze/please protocol of the reptilian brain, in a sociopathic state an individual or country will betray their own and all humanity out of instinctive, fearful reactions to manage the traumatic state. This includes suicide, addiction, betrayal, theft, rape, murder, and lies, both rational and irrational.

An empathic human being is traumatized by the trauma of another human being. They are further traumatized by sociopathic responses to others in trauma, such as: "They are the enemy. It's none of your business. It's not our problem. They deserve it. They are bad people." When the pain of empathizing with someone who is not getting help from the surrounding culture becomes so painful it prevents survival functions, a human being cuts off their empathy in order to cope, becoming sociopathic in the same instant to their own and other people's pain. This is how the sociopathic state spreads like a virus in times of human incompetence when the painful fruits of that incompetence become too much to bear.

The reptilian brain is 1000 times less effective at generating sustainable well-being than a rational empath, making it the single most important challenge for the species to increase the level of competence to a level where trauma and PTSD are reduced to a point where the vast majority of people are engaging as rational empaths, who will naturally work at reducing the trauma of the remaining minority of people.

A good analogy for the shift from sociopath to rational empath is a computer. Every time you type "Trauma" into the keyboard, the computer shuts down, reboots, and runs in diagnostic mode until the trauma has been located and resolved. While it is in diagnostic mode it is 1000 times slower than when it is in optimal mode. As soon as the trauma is resolved by a traumatically literate culture, it goes back to devoting its full resources to creating sustainable well-being.

The pivot point between these two worlds and between a human animal and a human being is traumatic literacy, a subset of psychological literacy. Updating the cultural software from traumatic illiteracy to traumatic literacy is one of the single most potent investments of energy the human body is capable of doing.

To update your software to traumatic literacy, read or listen to The Body Keeps the Score, and measure your effectiveness as a student by the changes you make in your life in response.

THE MOST SIGNIFICANT EQUATION

What is the biggest source of both human well-being and human suffering? Human behavior. What is the biggest source of human behavior? Human thought. Our intelligence can be measured by the percentage of our thoughts that results in behavior that generates feelings of well-being.

Let's review the biggest causes of human suffering:

- Depression.
- Disabilities of all kinds.
- Boredom.
- Shame.
- Trauma/PTSD.
- Hunger.
- Heart disease.
- Cancer.
- Health-care "complications."
- Betrayal.
- Loneliness.
- Lies.
- Sexual frustration.
- Nuclear threats.
- Pollution of our bodies, air, soil and water.
- Theft.
- Killing, at a personal or global scale.
- Food poisoning.
- Poor workmanship.
- Unsatisfying jobs.

- Corruption and abuse of power.
- Rape.
- Unfulfilling relationships.
- Low parenting skills.
- Bullying.
- Racism, Sexism, and all the isms.
- Incompetence.
- Global warming.
- Disposing of "garbage."
- Poor education.

Pick any one of these and ask yourself how big of an impact individual and collective human thought, words, feelings, and behavior has on creating both the reality in which the suffering is occurring and the degree of suffering an individual experiences within that reality? Make a list of all the ways that different human beings could, if they chose, dramatically reduce suffering for a human being in that area. I'll look at a few areas below:

- Let's take Joe, who just lost his wife July to Cancer, and is now sitting alone watching TV and thinking it might be better to numb out with alcohol or just kill himself rather than go through life alone. What can we do differently as a culture to reduce the odds of things getting to this point and respond to Joe if it does?

    - First, exercise, an enjoyable life, healthy organic food, minimizing exposure to chemicals, and incentivizing doctors to prevent and educate clients, rather than spend as little time as possible with clients are all things that have some likelihood of preventing or slowing down July's Cancer. Paying doctors more money the more medical treatment their patients require is a backward incentive.

- Universal health-care can make the focus less about money and more about enjoying the final days with a loved one.
- High schools that teach friendship-building and maintaining, the importance of co-creating healthy relationships, and how to be good neighbors would statistically reduce the odds that Joe is alone, with his spouse as his sole-confidant.
- Governments, based on science, rather than politics, would never have left millions of its citizens to face death in terror, with all psychoactive plants made illegal. Instead, routine use of psychoactive mushrooms, MDMA, and other compounds would be encouraged, based on their results, in easing transitions with a calm and healing death.
- Neighbors in a culture built on empathy would all gather to support Joe for a year after the death of his wife, helping him play a useful role in the neighborhood.
- Joe, in a culture free of the shame of need, would ask for the help he needed and might actually grow more after shedding an old identity and turning his attention to new things.
- A culture that respected elders and looked to them to mentor the young, would provide an opportunity for Joe to contribute his skills to the neighborhood and provide guidance to the young and a reason for Joe to keep living.

The gap between our millions of lonely seniors and many healthier and happier alternatives is big. However, there is nothing stopping us as individuals or in groups of one hundred people from choosing a 10 X better neighborhood experience. It's vastly easier if these habits are already part of the default in the neighborhood, but any two neighbors can adopt them and immediately experience higher well-being, lower risks, better health, and better support. They can save money by sharing tips, co-owning rarely used tools, and helping each other rather than hiring things out. It is cheaper, easier, more intelligent and more fun to be better neighbors than our culture produces statistically with its protocols. The only people that can change these protocols are us, individually and collectively.

There is not a single area of the statistically average life that could not easily become 1000% more intelligent if we made the effort individually and/or collectively. The fact that a majority will defend the status quo and block most change simply highlights the reality that human beings, by holding on to old habits of thinking, feeling, speaking, doing, and being, control most of their reality and are the only ones who can change it. In search of intelligence, change is necessary. This breaks down into two probable paths: top-down efforts to force people to change and individuals freely choosing to adopt a more intelligent pattern of living of their own initiative. Many do-good individuals and groups, confronted with the vast sea of human ignorance and apathy, have turned to violence, intimidation, laws, fines, and imprisonment to force change. In some cases, this is better than nothing. In many cases, the psychological mechanics that generate a backlash and resistance to all coercion makes this "medicine" worse than the disease. By the time we have a police state simply so that people will "volunteer" not to litter; we have a bigger problem than litter.

We can then look to the question: What do parents, a teacher, or a friend have to do in order to inspire an interest in living a high-quality life consistent with a 10 X lifestyle? That is what this book is all about.

There are two pivot points on the path to a 10 X reality without coercion:

- The first is traumatic literacy, leading to prevention and repair of PTSD, such that the default operating system of a given individual or group is human and empathic, rather than sociopathic and reptilian. Every traumatized person lives in fear and acts out of fear of being punished for doing the "wrong" thing." By becoming personally literate in the arena of trauma and PTSD through such books as The Body Keeps the Score, and helping others to do the same, you can free up the blood to flow into the human brain. As long as trauma, shame, and sociopathic behavior are active, blood will flow to the reptilian/fear-based brain and even "good" behavior will be done primarily out of fear.

- If you are able to bring a small group of people into an empathic state, free of trauma and the reptilian reactions it produces, you have created an ethical, motivated operating system that is creative and open to change. This is by far the most difficult step in a culture that is trauma-illiterate. Less than one in ten people around us can explain what trauma is, how it affects the brain and body, and what to do to prevent it from becoming PTSD or cure PTSD when it does. This means that most of us are relying on the sociopathic brain made vastly smarter by the rational brain. The rational reptile can make money; kill people, steal, or look good in public. It cannot empathize love and does not know what a human being is, other than someone to exploit.

- The second step is easy after the first step: Provide knowledge of best-practices in the areas that matter. Here are a few areas where best practices matter:

  - How do you have a good fight with your partner that leads to a healthier marriage?
  - How do you provide more value to your client and make more money?
  - How do you care for your body to live an optimal life?
  - How to drive ten times safer?
  - How to create a satisfying sexual relationship that is win/win?

Let's say that you work with a small group of people and succeed in fulfilling each of your human needs and healing the PTSD in your body, freeing your body r to allow the empathic brain to orient thinking, feeling, speaking, doing, and being on the axis of empathy for oneself, other humans and the larger ecology. This automatically motivates each individual in an empathic state to want what is "good, beautiful, and true" for themselves, others, and our environment. If this intention is refined with attention to detail, it will lead to a hunger for understanding best-practices and applying them. No empathic contractor will ignore best safety practices for their employees and no empathic employee will install something that saves them a few minutes of time but hurts the client a lot in the future. Empathy begins with the question "What is best for all in this situation?" From there it is a matter of understanding: learning how and why one approach is better than another for creating a better world.

In a largely sociopathic environment, safety begins by creating a circle: a safe space within which to develop and open the empathic brain. This is, in essence, a ritual with an unspoken sub-text that goes something like this: "I/we gather here today for the purpose of creating a more empathic world. We trust those in this circle to mean no harm to others in the circle and to honor the protocols we establish for safety here today." This container, when created well, provides the relaxation necessary to drop down into a deeper connection with others in the circle. It is the first step in a 10 X Life and, as others join in, a 10 X World.

Data about best-practices is abundant: Around the world, competent human beings have measured what works and observed results and are happy to share this information. However, many of the best practices cost less money than far inferior practices and products. In a sociopathic paradigm, this incentivizes companies with inferior, more expensive products and services to direct clients to their door with ads telling half and misleading truths. By contrast, the lowest priced products and services tend to have no budget for advertising. The same is true for government propaganda: you don't need to spend billions to brainwash a population into doing something that is in their interest. You do need to spend that kind of money to turn a population of sheep into people willing to follow the herd without doing their own research. This is also why it is far more difficult to discover and to implement best-practices while using the sociopathic operating system. Everyone knows how to help a molested child, allow a homeless person to secure a warm place to sleep and understand that having soda and fast-food at school rather than wholesome food and water is bad for the well-being of children and their education. It is simply that when combining all of the bribes, kick-backs, political deals, and ignorance of certain demographics it is "profitable" to do the wrong thing. A small group of people who put public interest above all other agendas can easily discern the best research and practices world-wide and attempt to share them. The public will have their ears full of advertising, smear campaigns, and lies to drown them out by companies protecting profits made by selling inferior practices.

It is a major accomplishment to bring a single human being into an empathic state, aware of the threats and reality of sociopathic protocols within the cult-ure, and aware of the best practices available to them to shape their lives. It might take $150,000. in therapies, investments, courses, and books to do so; money well spent for roughly 1% of the population. The most intelligent question is how to bring the cost of time, money, and natural resources down by 90% to $15,000. Is there a way that a human being in most of the countries on earth could get there ten times faster and ten times cheaper?

Bring a human being into a state of empathy and then empower them with the information needed to express that empathy potently through best-practices and we accelerate the path to an optimal future while avoiding the many pitfalls of using force to compel behavior and the vertical relationships required to do so. This is the path of grace in the direction of beauty, truth, and goodness.

I invite you to explore a set of protocols optimized for stimulating, healing, and nurturing the empathic brain in togetherness:

https://www.10xliving.org/dimensions

CHANGING MEMES FOR PENNIES

What is the cheapest way to change human thought? We are spending over twenty trillion dollars a year as a species in ways that make our personal and ecological lives worse, due to suboptimal thoughts. How much time and money is it worth spending to reduce that amount to spending only one to two trillion to make our lives worse? Is it worth two hundred billion?

These are the hurdles we have to face to get to nirvana: The state in which everyone on the planet can learn in minutes what the best way to achieve personal and ecological well-being is, in their situation in the current paradigm:

- The first hurdle is that only the top 5% in any arena follow best-practices. Those that don't follow best-practices will go bankrupt if they say "I'm not part of the 5%" so they try and muddy the water, rather than ceding credibility to the top 5%.
- If the top 5% are identified and communicate through mainstream media, they will always advocate for major changes, since the bottom 90% of people are using vastly inefficient protocols that are usually outdated and sometimes even destructive to the goal.
- This will upset advertisers and special interest groups, who can hire "experts" and ads to black-list the most competent people, confusing the public.
- The public, by definition, does not have the skill to be in the top 5% so does not know who is right, and follows the herd. So we keep smoking for decades while there is "no proven link between cancer," we keep addicting the population to opioids as "not addictive" and keep lead in our gasoline for almost a century, killing millions.

When there is a bottleneck on expensive media, paid by advertisers and regulated by the government, the public will hear what their government and the largest advertisers want them to hear, because news agencies such as WikiLeaks will be illegally hunted down by governments and media that tells the truth will be boycotted by advertisers until they go out of business or can't hire the best talent and the public goes elsewhere. Any media organization that gets too big is offered threats and bribes until their integrity gets worn down and any politician that gets too powerful is given the same treatment. The concentrated approach to distributing information is incapable of transcending the reptilian brain and is capable of killing the stories that matter most to human lives.

This leads us to decentralized data, generated by individuals and digested by individuals without any censorship. This takes us into several directions:
- Decentralized global blockchains that no one government can dominate.
- Individual encryption that prevents harassment of individuals by the government.
- Data entered on personal cell-phones in private areas.
- The technology is within the umbrella of a non-profit entity.
- Keeping costs very low to avoid financial dependency.

Having a clear and accurate picture of probabilities based on unbiased data that has been entered by individuals with no financial agenda is the single best way to earn trust in the data. Having trust in the data is critical if we are to make decisions that increase our short-term discomfort while leading to global well-being.

The data that is most relevant for health and well-being of all kinds is meta-data shared by individuals around the world. If I know for certain that someone of my age range and blood type has a 60% chance of doing well with drug A and a 70% chance of doing well with drug B with my condition, I don't need to worry about who has bribed my doctor to push drug A, or which revolving government/pharmaceutical company doors lead to a drug being approved by my government health agency. Nor will there be a political divide around the data. The media may take bribes to attack the data, but that will simply lead to a decline in ad-based media, as people have an alternate source of truth.

For meta-data to be free, or low-cost, it must be voluntarily given. In a culture that is 60% self-centered/sociopathic, the hurdle to overcome is this: Why would you or I voluntarily share a piece of data about our lives that will become aggregated as meta-data in a non-profit dissemination device?

Let's look at what might make you share personal info:

We have to start by eliminating fears and resistance:

- No one wants personal information shared publicly.
- No one wants to worry about legal or other hassles because they shared something about their lives.
- No one wants to be deluged by ads, using private information.
- No one wants to be judged.
- No one wants to share information that will make a few people rich who will sell their data.
- Most people don't want to do things to "help others" that do not benefit themselves first.
- No one wants to change their habits unless there is a compelling reason to do so.

A non-profit app that turned all personal data into meta-data, was hosted on a block-chain, was deeply encrypted, and free to download and use addresses most of these issues. However, we have to look at why you would be excited to enter the data that would make the database the most valuable database the species has ever created:

- The first thing is curiosity: We are very curious about anything that a lot of people are talking about and so will give anything a try once if there is a lot of buzz about it. This project is so rare that it would receive the global attention necessary to generate this buzz.
- The second thing is personal curiosity: People are deeply moved by learning how they are different and similar to other people. Here are questions everyone wants to know and which cannot be answered currently:
    - What percentage of people in my town have cancer?
    - What percentage of people in my town is afraid of losing their housing?
    - What percentage of people in my town want the local parks to get more funding?
    - How many people would like a new Italian Restaurant if I want to start one?
    - How many people are lonely and want to find a way to connect?
    - How many people in my town are bothered by loud mufflers?
    - What is the best way people in my age group in my town are meeting each other?
- We have an endless degree of curiosity about things we currently have no data about. Even if we can find out some of these things, the wasted time sorting through click-bait on Google is mind-numbing.

Quid pro quo: A free exchange of information. We all have so many questions about ourselves and each other. No one wants to fill out a survey for information gathered by a stranger or someone we don't know that will be published months later and cost a lot of money to produce for someone else's agenda. However, what if in order to see the information you want to know, you must become a participant, question by question? Here's how it works:

- If you type in "What is the most beautiful hike in my town?" you will be asked two questions before getting the answer:
    - How avid and experienced a hiker are you in your town 1-10?
    - What is your favorite place to hike?
- As soon as you click "submit" you will instantly see the statistics based on other's answers:
    - "70% of people voted this hike as the number one hike with 50 people voting as of now."
    - 20% of people voted this hike to be the number one hike with 50 people voting as of now.
    - 10% of people voted this other hike the best hike with 50 people voting as of now.
    - Check back a year later and the answers may have changed as more people ask and answer the question.
- Now imagine 1000 different questions you may want to ask and are required to answer, any time you are curious about where the most crimes are being committed, where traffic is worst at what times, or the favorite location in ten miles for a romantic dinner.

All thought is composed in language. The best way to think clearer is to write things down. As you clarify, with writing, your answer to a wide variety of questions, your thinking will improve with complete confidentiality. No one is going to argue with you about your favorite restaurant. You won't be glared at by the sloppy waiter you put up with at a restaurant with great food and poor service because the votes are aggregated anonymously, and because the voting cannot be hacked by multiple accounts. By requiring comments to be made by phones that are in the area they are commenting on (no hiring out to another country for 50 positive votes on a crappy restaurant) and linked to a fingerprint sign-in, to avoid bot accounts, this becomes the most objective database without political overtones.

Another feature you might explore is "What are the questions most of the people in my town, city, or country are asking?" You might read through, find some you are curious about and click on that question. Before you can read what anyone else thinks, you must answer the question yourself, after which you can see if you are in the majority or minority opinion. This creates a fascinating opportunity to evaluate our positions and perspectives, relative to others.

How much does it cost to answer 1000 questions relevant to your well-being and interests, and learn from others who answered the same question? Perhaps $10. per year in data-storage per person. However, from that database, you can get real up-to-date unbiased pictures of what's going on in different regions of the world with complete privacy. This allows important conversations to take place publicly about the meta-data that would be difficult to have between individuals who answer in particular ways that can be shamed in public.

- Let's say you have a 25% nicer romantic dinner for your anniversary because you took three minutes to enter and explore the topic. That cost you less than a penny.
- Let's say you learned about a 30% better chiropractor for a herniated disk by asking that question specifically and going there (some chiropractors are good at some things and not others) and again spent one penny.
- Let's say you feel 30% less lonely by understanding why others in your neighborhood are lonely as well and what to do about it and take three steps to reduce your loneliness for another penny, living a 5% longer lifespan as a result of reducing your loneliness. That cost you a penny as well.

- Let's say you ask "how to talk to my son about being sexually safe" and find out how to form a closer bond, rather than humiliate him and stop talking. That costs a penny as well but is priceless in its health and family benefits.

Best practices are always evolving over time as we learn better ways of doing things. Traditionally, it takes a generation for each iteration because gathering and sharing information statistically is so expensive, biased, and takes so long. Imagine if you could get the latest protocols in minutes on anything important to you, not just from your area, but from all around the world. This is a big deal, as anyone who travels a lot knows that every place on earth does some things better than the rest of the world but locals all over the world do what their parents did, not what the parents of more talented cultures are doing and have been doing for years. This leverages the entire species for best practices, breaking through cultural and geographic barriers.

THE MOST VALUABLE DATABASE

If you had access to the most valuable database on earth, would you want it? What data would be on the most valuable database on earth? Our first impulse might be to imagine a database of stocks that were guaranteed to 10 X over the next year. Nothing could be more simple than the theory that becoming rich would solve all our problems. Then we could be happy. This is what is called "cult dogma." We live in a cult that states that we should spend 80% of our time preparing for work and then working at jobs we often don't like because then we can have money and then we will be happy. Dogmas are so immune to data that they continue in the face of facts. We believe in the dogma and show our faith by picking more money over many other choices.

For those wishing to question our cult dogmas around money here are a few data points:

- Happiness increases going from no money to around $70k per year - the point at which a typical westerner can meet all their basic needs and have a little left over. It does not increase much, if at all, going over that point unless it ties in with a strong purpose or vision that requires more than that.
- Most Americans will choose to work an hour of overtime per day and get one less hour of sleep but an extra hour of sleep will make most Americans happier than the money with the over time.
- 50% of billionaires are just as unhappy as the typical person and many are more so.
- Three years after winning the lottery many winners are less happy than they were before winning.

- Happiness often goes down after life becomes too comfortable and we stop growing due to having achieved our financial goals.
- Most people pretend that the answer to these statistics is simply to pursue even more money, never reaching the point where they feel enough.
- Healthy daily routines and meaningful relationships do affect happiness enormously and have very little to do with money.
- What a majority of people do for the primary purpose of making money leads to high levels of stress, frustration, boredom, addiction, and loneliness.

Money in and of itself has zero value. It is a symbol of value, and the ultimate value is a high level of sustainable well-being. The most valuable database is one that facilitates sustainable well-being. This includes:

- Best-practices: ways of doing things that bring about the most value with the least amount of unnecessary suffering.
- The most efficient ways to sustainably respond to problems and pains we are experiencing at that time.
- The people with the skills and resources to maximize our odds of fun and success.

Imagine a database of probable responses to the overwhelm of getting cancer and seeing this:

- 90% of people in your generation, sharing your gender and living within two hundred miles find this to be the best response to the overwhelm of a cancer diagnosis…
- If that does not work, 70% of people find this to be the best response….
- If that does not work, 65% of people find this to be the best response…

- Here are the personal stories of people who have navigated this territory, including these three who are willing to be mentors for you. Here are their stories…

Once key sources of pain are mastered, what's your most important goal? The answer to that question might be informed by looking at the statistics of the goal that, when accomplished by people like you, had the single biggest impact on increasing the well-being in their lives. Imagine learning that an hour of jogging, when introduced, did more for the overall well-being of people like you than anything that cost money. These people might not even know that jogging was indirectly responsible for better marriages by exhausting irritation in the body, better sex lives, and greater physical happiness, leading to higher levels of self-esteem.

If I want to learn a new language, then I want to know the protocol people like me use to learn it faster and more reliably than any other way. If I want to meet and build friendships, I want to know the most likely way to do that, based on what's working for people in my age range and area. If I have a headache, I'd like to know the things that have worked best for the most people.

The best way… The easiest way… The cheapest way to achieve the things most correlated with reduced suffering and sustainable well-being is based on statistics and personal stories from the people around me. That's the most valuable database I can imagine! Right now, it does not exist, so the key question is "how can it be created?"

TEMPLATE FOR A 10 X NON PROFIT

A 10 X Non Profit must gather time, money, and natural resources ten times more efficiently than average, organize these patterns of energy intelligently, and use them to produce more sustainable human well-being for more people than the status quo by a 1000% margin.

Although the only goal that matters is generating 1000% more sustainable well-being per unit of energy invested, relative to average, the following micro-goals and protocols point in the general direction of success:

- Lower the cost of raising money and overhead: According to this website (https://doublethedonation.com/nonprofit-fundraising-statistics/) 10-85% of most non-profit money is spent fundraising and on administration with an average range being 15-25%. To beat this statistic and lower costs by 90% we would need to hit 2 3% total overhead. Protocols for lowering overhead:
    - Encouraging checks over credit cards.
    - Lobbying credit cards to eliminate 2.5% fees for non-profits.
    - Stay small and volunteer: I volunteer 100% of my time to my non-profit and am currently the only donor. As a result, I spend zero money fundraising and zero money goes to credit cards. Since it's my money and my time I am highly motivated to see that each penny is spent efficiently to maximize well-being. I also enjoy giving more when I can see the results first-hand.
    - I run four non-profits and contribute less than $50,000. per year to each. This avoids 100% of the accounting and tax costs for the non-

profit and makes the start-up process cost less than $1,000. per non-profit.
- The smaller a non-profit, the more efficiently it can be run. Grant-writers, secretaries, software programs, an office, staff, contractors to fix problems in the office, equipment, and more are all eliminated with a small non-profit.
- Having a tax-free investment account also provides the possibility for the non-profit to make more money than it spends in a given year, without taxes on profits. This further reduces dependency on fundraising efforts. By investing in companies such as Tesla, manufacturer of the most energy-efficient car-company on earth, as well as the safest cars in the world, my non-profit can make a return on investment while supporting cleaner air and longer life for drivers.

- Develop 10 times better ideas for organizing these resources:
  - Before starting my non-profit, I spent thirty days during which I would spend 30 minutes a day and up to $30. making people happier in the most efficient way that I knew how. One day I cleaned garbage on a beach in thirty minutes. Another day I took a Thai friend to the dentist. One of my ideas was to start a non-profit so I would not need to pay taxes on the things I was doing for public benefit. I think this exercise is a good place to start. I'd love to hear your favorite idea for bringing about sustainable happiness for $30. and a half hour of your time: dane@happinessdata.org

- Leverage these ideas 10 times more through partnerships: If you find a way to bring about high levels of well-being sustainably, you may not be able to do all of it yourself or with the non-profit you are associated with. It makes sense to partner with other non-profits and individuals to share ideas and fund those that have the greatest benefit. That's what this book is for me – a way to share my research and experience with others. This book helps sharpen my ideas, gives me something to aim towards, and allows me to talk with you for $4.00 per printed book with postage. If you spend $10,000. 30% more intelligently because of this $4.00 investment in our dialog which means $4.00 turns into $3,000. more well-being in the world because of you.

- Focus on root issues of suffering to preempt problems that are 10 times more expensive to solve than they are to prevent: Trauma becoming PTSD is a great example. After spending $100k on various psychotherapies, only to discover that talk-therapy is not effective for treating Complex PTSD, I realized that my therapists lacked the competency to diagnose and respond. However, I did not realize their incumbency until multiple therapists got poor results over a ten year period responding to symptoms of PTSD. In my case, PTSD developed several hours after multiple traumas went un-treated. It would have been free to stop the traumas from happening, which were preventable, and about thirty minutes of a competent adult's time to stop the trauma from crystalizing into an identity of PTSD. Those missing thirty minutes of competency have left me with a PTSD identity for decades. This has made it harder for people to get close to me, reduced my well-being in the most idyllic circumstances, and cost me 50% of the well-being I might naturally have experienced. In short, preventing trauma for free and preventing trauma from becoming PTSD is one of the most efficient ways I know to reduce and prevent chronic suffering in the world. Since PTSD leads to a shortened lifespan, increased heart-failure, and higher rates of depression, addiction, and divorce, it is a root problem that creates too many problems. Removing the root eliminates many other problems that can take longer to fix.

- Compete based on data to provide more value per unit of energy than any other organization in history: The reptilian brain is competitive so use that drive to the benefit of your non-profit. Aim to be the best at delivering a pound of well-being for an ounce of time, money, and natural resources and measure it. One of the legitimate criticisms of non-profits is that by relying on donors and not measuring key results per dollar, they are less efficient than Walmart or Costco at delivering efficient value.

- Must make it ten times easier for people to contribute their time than a traditional non-profit: What non-profit do you know that bothers to understand your passion, skills, resources, and competencies? What if you have an idea for reducing spending in the office of a non-profit? What if you are one of the best animal trainers in the world? What if you love painting and can make art for an auction? Most non-profits don't know and don't utilize the real talents of their volunteers, offering low-skill chores that anyone can do to talented people. It's stupid when you realize that someone might have the skill to contribute $1,000. in value with their time but only feel comfortable giving $300. of their cash. Figure out a way to tap into this resource and challenge people to develop their skills and interests still further, leaving them better able to generate value in the world after they are done volunteering. Make sure you have a way for people to propose projects and get them done that they are capable of doing.

- Measure your impact in personal ways over time: So you helped Mark regain his hearing. Can he make a video about this on an app that does not require you to spend $200. with your webpage builder to "highlight." Can he check in and share what he is experiencing a year later, outlining what things are possible because he has his hearing back?

- Open source your non-profit operating system, with all its failures and successes so that other non-profits can follow the 10 X protocol: Highlight your biggest mistakes and biggest wins so that as many people as possible can copy what works and avoid what does not. Pair up with at least five other non-profits who want to teach and be taught what works. The best non-profits put growth and results ahead of ego and will jump at the chance. The worst non-profits will sell out their mission to avoid the shame of sharing mistakes and are not ideal teachers you can learn from.

10 X IDEA

An open-source Decentralized Autonomous Organization (DAO) is among the most powerful structures for organizing as a species because, much like bitcoin, no government can control it and no personality can dominate it over time. Open-sourced, data-based, competent democracies are needed to assist the species to evolve. The structure for this project is a global DAO based on Ethereum code.

The Idea:

Harness the information in the world to accelerate intelligent cultural decision-making in 10%-80% of the world's population through a combination of personal and meta-data with well-being as the primary objective.

A Bit of Perspective:

No one on the planet knows how I'm feeling today. No one knows why I'm feeling what I feel. You don't. To some extent, I don't. The U.S. government does not have a clue. My local mayor does not know. It's astonishing that not a single entity on the planet knows how I'm feeling today, what I'm thinking about, what my goals are, what my schedule is, or most of the other relevant things in my life.

This is factually profound: Not one agency, government, company, or non-profit, and possibly not a single person knows these things about you either. Think about that for a moment: For most of the world's population, not a single person knows most of the data that is most relevant to human well-being. The data that is known is outdated almost as soon as it is gathered, costs millions of dollars to gather, and is fragmented at best.

Leverage:

Quest: What is the single most powerful way to change the world?

Answer: Change the decision-making pattern of human beings.

Quest: What is the most efficient sustainable way to change the decision-making pattern of human beings?

Answer:
- Reduce levels of trauma, fear, and pain so that fear of change and the unknown is reduced, freeing up the rational brain.
- Provide accurate, relevant data to people's rational brain in the form they need to digest it.

Quest: What is the most cost-effective, timely, and scalable way to get information and share information as a species?

Answer: Mobile phones.

What emerges is a clear direction:

To gather the nuanced information about every person's personal well-being as data and meta-data, synthesize that data into useful patterns and correlations a rational brain can understand, and share that information instantly and freely with anyone who wants it.

Making the most valuable app in the world:
- Available in any language with built in translation.

- Available to download from the web and all platforms that will host it so it cannot be controlled.
- The data-base of the app is block-chain based in every country.
- The primary currency of the app is Bitcoin.
- The best encryption in the world with people able to answer all questions as personal data or meta-data, resulting in higher levels of honesty with less political repercussions.
- Before any individual can access meta-data and data about a topic, they must answer the questions as data or meta-data relevant to that topic.
- The core use of the app is free with no ads.
- The app measures trustworthiness in 75 distinct areas over time, allowing people to predict statistically what our impact on them will be when they interact with us. For example, if we are 10 minutes late to 50% of our appointments, all the people setting appointments with us will see that and know how to prepare.
- Each app user controls 100% of their information associated with their profile and what happens to it.
- The app randomizes and shares all information as meta-data grouped by regions of roughly 100 square miles so that useful insight can be gathered about patterns of thinking, feeling, speaking, doing, and being per town or area while protecting privacy.
- The app consists of roughly 1000 data-points per person in the areas that matter most to human and planetary well-being.
- The app aims to be the single most useful app in the world for:
  - Gaining employment based on true fit in personality, preference, and competency.
  - Participating in a variety of DAO's around the world.
  - Learning what one's strengths are and documenting those.
  - Forming meaningful, long-term relationships based on trust and competency.

- Creating smart contracts on a block-chain with meta-data about those smart contracts and lifetime recourse.
- Creating an unfakable identity consisting of iris, face, finger-print, voice, long-term patterns, and feedback from others.
- Buying, giving, receiving, trading, and selling any resource we want or have more efficiently than any marketplace in the world.
- Investing time, money, and natural resources we control in a better future, as we define that.
- Helping each other in crisis.
- Getting rapid accurate data about any topic relevant to human well-being.
- Share best practices for using any technology to achieve any goal with constant iterative up-voting by the most competent people on the planet.
- Become a block-chain voting and meta-voting vehicle for every value, political candidate, and election on the planet.
- Create personal searches using AI and highly customizable criteria to create a 10 X better search engine than Google is today.
- Create a market for trust-based, value-based investing on an individual level.
- Create the best crowd-funding platform on the planet, allowing people to fund with time, resources, money, connection, and voting.
- Create a decision-making module that weights:
    - Competence.
    - Skin in the game.
    - Trustworthiness.
    - Supporting data.
- Makes buying non-profit deliverables accountable and data driven around the world:
    - "This is the cheapest place to buy a square foot of rainforest anywhere on the planet."

- "This is the cheapest doctor to give $4. to in order to cure a child's cataracts anywhere in the world."
  - "This sexual abuse clinic helps more people per dollar with higher victim praise than any sexual abuse clinic in the country."
  - In short, creating an Amazon marketplace for worthy causes.
- Create a guaranteed right to be on the platform with each person free to block contact from any other person and some trust-data mandatory to be transparent.

The Network Effect:

Information leading to the enhanced ability to predict the future, create, co-create, and distribute well-being is the most valuable human asset in the world. No one is doing even 1/10th of the work needed to gather and share this information with the world's population. Its value is unleashed by the network effect.

The Most Powerful Network Drivers:

Every for-profit company can be sued by shareholders for not prioritizing return on investment. Most executives are driven by quarterly bets. A bet like this is a fifty year bet, with ten years of legwork before results become clear. This creates a tremendous conflict of interest that a DAO non-profit does not have to deal with. This same DAO generates tremendous value for the users:

1. Twitter, Facebook, and YouTube have all deplatformed individuals for questionable reasons. A data-base of people and data that no one will ever be de-platformed from is unique and increases the platform's value.
2. Curiosity leads people to want to answer questions so that they can view the statistical meta-data relevant to that same question.

3. A DAO guarantees freedom of speech and purer information that is trans-cultural. This will be very magnetic.
4. This project is uniquely relevant to every human on the planet and will likely generate more than $1 billion in free media promotions around the world.
5. A decentralized open-source software protocol with competency up-voting that ensures that the most competent people have 100 times the voting influence of the uneducated will lead to the software continually iterating in response to up-voting.
6. The ability for anyone to add value to the app and have that validated directly by the user will encourage massive participation.
7. Self-awareness and education without advertising is a human need that is currently only met around 2% in the world.
8. The ability to accept donations in Bitcoin and channel that money transparently to improve the app and to help those most in need most efficiently will generate goodwill.
9. Crowd-funded species projects such as:
    a. An asteroid defense system for the planet.
    b. Colonizing the moon and Mars.
    c. Creating a 10 X Country floating on the world's greatest Ocean garbage dump that recycles and reuses all that plastic.
    d. These types of projects can be set up as DAO, funded on the blockchain by the world community and everyone can be a part of it. This creates buzz, meaning, excitement, and the need to participate.
10. The DAO nature of the organization and app will transcend race and country to some extent, allowing anyone best able to play a role to do so remotely as long as they play that role better than anyone else who wants to play the role. In this way, the best people in the world will play the roles outlined in the DAO structure.

11. The Feedback Module: The ability to capture real-time feedback 10 times more easily about what users like and dislike about every page on the app, as well as to prioritize feedback by competent users over incompetent users, and up-vote ideas made by users ensures that the most important suggestions and ideas people care about will be up-voted, and the app will be constantly iterated to include the top idea until it is implemented, at which point it will shift to the next top idea in a democracy of competent voting, ensuring that the developers will always be focusing on what people care about. The feedback module as a 10 X experience is among the most important features of the app.
12. The ability to do smart-contracts with any amount of money for loans, investments, gifts, and companies will make the app highly relevant for inter-personal banking - replacing banks more efficiently than any bank is run today.

PATHWAYS TO REALITY

The fact that one man can visualize, grasp, outline, and communicate an idea that could start with as little as $750,000 in seed capital and could have more impact than any venture in human history means that this idea will happen. The question is simply when. The fact that information is the most valuable asset on the planet means that the entity can self-generate as much money as it needs once the network effect is created.

We are at the gateway of transcendence. Any millionaire on the planet could realize this picture three years ago. However, it's not clear how doing so would be immediately gratifying to the reptilian brain. Fear, short-term thinking, greed, and shame have wiped this out as an actuality.

With transcendent consciousness, it becomes the most powerful inevitability and priority. This speaks to the power of the transcendent regions of the brain to release a level of sustainable human well-being and ecological sustainability that we can only hint at today.

Myself: I am investing in Bitcoin, Tesla, my landscape company, and more to create $750,000. to fund the first step in this project: A 10 X Landscape App that can generate the yearly revenues needed to grow this entity.

Happiness Data: As the chairman of www.HappinessData.org, a 501c3 I can also promote this idea and invite $1 million in funding to make it a full-time idea to get off the ground and into an international DAO structure after developing the app personally with a built in feedback module to iterate all of my ideas and add many more.

DIRECTIONS TO AIM FOR

- **Transparency:** Transparency leads to collaboration, attunement, responsiveness, and support for intelligent projects.

- **Blockchain:** When intelligent people have access to complete and accurate data, they make intelligent decisions. Data becomes the enemy of intelligent people when it is incomplete or distorted for political purposes. Establishing data on a decentralized block-chain shifts focus away from "who is most effective at suppressing aspects of the data" to "who is more effective at aligning their protocols with accurate data."

- **A Competence Democracy:** An ignorant crowd does more harm than an informed benevolent dictator. The most competent people in any field are always a minority consisting of less than 2% of the field. The single most important step in extraordinary success is selecting for high competency. The only people capable of doing this are other highly competent people in this minority. Finding the first person in this group - who will always be somewhat at odds with the status quo - is the beginning. The weight of a vote on decisions in a given field needs to be based on competency, not numbers. However, to avoid civil war, competency must be paired with education in a format the majority can understand and try out for themselves.

- **Generating Useful Data:** If I have a concern about air quality, rising sea levels, and global warming, the intelligent response is to take some action, such as buying an acre of rain-forest to donate for preservation in a forest that might otherwise be logged. If I know where the cheapest acre of rainforest is on the planet, I can buy it in a matter of minutes by sending bitcoin to the non-profit that has negotiated a 10,000 acre purchase as a lease/option at a rate of $300. per acre. I click "send" and get a $300. tax write off, and an acre is saved cheaper than any other place on the planet. However, I don't have that information. I don't have any of the most essential information organized for efficient investment in my own or the planet's well-being. Creating that information and bringing it to people's phones is the most highly leveraged activity any enterprise can be involved in. It is enormously motivating to know with certainty that the money we invest is going to be used extremely effectively.

- **Meeting Human Needs:** To statistically move a population from the operating system of a reptile or a human animal to an empathic, intelligent human being, involves systematically ensuring that the survival, security, love, and belonging needs of every person in that population are met. As soon as this is done, the cost of managing sociopathic, reptilian behavior drops by 80% or more, allowing that energy to be redirected to meet those needs profitably. In other words, when one 1% of the population using a sociopathic operating system requires 99% of the population to spend 30% of their energy in defense and it takes only 10% of a population's energy to ensure that every person meets their needs to survive, feel secure and have high levels of love and belonging, it is both ignorant and in-efficient to uphold cultural dogmas of individual responsibility that guaranty that a minority of the population will be highly traumatized and operate as reptiles.

- **Education:** Showing people the easiest path they can take to sustainably increase their personal well-being without harming others is the most highly leveraged useful activity. An intelligent person will always pick the easiest way of increasing their well-being if they know what that is. In areas where it appears that people are being destructive, it simply means that people do not understand the full complexity of the situation. For example, when trauma is not understood and responded to, there will be addicts. When addiction is not understood, it may appear that people are being destructive. Take away the trauma, heal the PTSD, and understand the benefits of compulsive behavior as short-term pain-management, and suddenly people appear to be what they always were: rational within the framework of their available choices and information.

- **A Focus on Results:** Everyone wants the same result: sustainable well-being efficiently generated for all. Reality will always be more complex than the story we tell to allow our minds to relate to reality. In highly traumatized cultures the fear of the unknown, correlating with the fear of being out of control, is very high, leading to an attachment to our story of events, even when that story is at odds with the data. This tension between reality and dogma leads to almost all intelligent innovations being attacked by a majority. In order to bypass this crucifixion of evolution, uncertainty, and change, there needs to be healthy competition on a level playing field based on results: "Can you take this group of 100 people and make them sustainably happier for $100?" Making "sense" is not as important as the data of impact.

- **Synergy:** Reducing the friction of search, communication, engagement, and partnering on projects of shared interest is the single most powerful technology the species can generate:
    - How can an individual who is competent and only speaks Russian, find and partner with another individual who only speaks English to have a powerful impact?

- How can one person's laptop sitting idly in Romania be loaded with an equation to solve for another group in England working on a weather-mapping model?
- How can an A.I. computer in Silicon Valley help a high school class in India answer the question: "What is the single most important thing our town can do to increase well-being over the next 30 years?"
- How can someone with a spare refrigerator they don't need transform that into a tax-free donation to their favorite charity with less hassle than hauling it to the dump?
- How can someone with knowledge that no one in a group likes or trusts share their knowledge to benefit a cause that helps everyone?
- What is the easiest bridge between two computer networks that would allow both networks to work together?
- How can I share $10,000. from 7pm-7am every night as a 12 hour micro-loan that leaves my account and returns to create liquidity for projects I want to help out?
- How can I allow someone I've never met before to stay in my house for free with complete security at the last minute so they can focus on doing something good for the world?

- **Healing Chauvinism:** In a stunning deviation from science and intelligence, many of the people with the most money and things feel more depressed and lonely than people with much less, while not knowing what to do about it. One can go cradle to grave in a "modern" culture without a single hour of emotional literacy based on science. Every single action in the history of the species is emotionally based, leading to the question: "If much of our lives are a direct result of our decisions, and all of our decisions are based on feelings we often do not understand, why isn't motivation and emotional science the single most important subject for parents, teachers, students, and employee/employers? Healing Chauvinism removes the bias against the inner world in favor of obsessing about the things that our thoughts, feelings, and decisions create.

- **The Science of Identity:** Each of us was born into a cult-ure, learning habits of thinking, feeling, speaking, doing, and being. Our personal identity, to a large extent, mirrors the cult-ural identity. What's missing is a data-based analysis of our cult-ure. A cult is an unexamined dogma that everyone is forced to adopt that is crazy (i.e. it wastes vast amounts of energy to make people feel worse than they would have felt without spending that energy). Of the 10,000 cult-ures in human history estimated to have existed, 95% of them are now extinct. In other words, our cult-ure has a 95% chance of changing so much in 1000 years that we can no longer recognize it or being extinct because there are far better ways of doing things than what we are doing today. To speed that evolutionary process along, we have to audit every aspect of our cult-ure to measure the amount of sustainable well-being yielded for each of our cult memes, and comparing these with audits of other cult-ures, past and present. Holding on to traditions that yield lower levels of well-being than other patterns of thinking, feeling, speaking, doing, and being is a trauma-coping mechanism for avoiding fear of the unknown, and its antidote is becoming traumatically and psychologically literate.

$1 BILLION SPENT INTELLIGENTLY

Most of us have a few thousand to a few million dollars we might give in service to humanity. As a result, we think of things that can be accomplished for that amount. Some of the most efficient ideas for realizing human well-being at a global level require a bigger vision. What would you do if you had a billion dollars and wanted to improve the sustainable welfare of humanity for the next thousand years?

Below, I explore my initial thoughts in response to this question. I'd love to hear your answer, if you will take the time to write it down.

Endowment: $89 million invested with a 10 year horizon so that the non-profit will never have to raise money again to function.

- $30 million invested in Ethereum.
- $5 million invested in Bitcoin.
- $30 million invested in Tesla and other Elon Musk companies.
- $10 million invested in new startups that can help the world and are having hard times getting funded due to short-term thinking.
- $5 million loaned to people with good ideas and a reasonable chance of paying it back.
- $9 million kept in appreciating cash equivalents such as gold.

The 10 X Non Profit Template: $30 Million

- Hire 20 staff at $120,000 from bright people in lower- income countries that support their families and give a good return for the non-profit.
- Develop a 10 X Non-Profit DAO: $1 million

- Develop an App that runs every aspect of the non-profit including donations and transparent spending: $750,000
- Invite 30 at a time from the biggest non-profits in the world to get together for 30 days by donation and learn to use the app and run a 10 X Non Profit.
- License the app to all non-profits for 5% of their gross revenue after showing that it cuts overhead by 70% or more, benefiting their causes.
- Provide seed-capital $5 million at a time to non-profits with 1% interest loans and consulting so they can be effective and then pay us back.
- Invest $10 million in long-term investments, such as Tesla, so there is tax-free income coming in.
- Hold yearly summits for ten days in which we:
  - Host all non-profits who wish to be there.
  - Invite anyone with a good idea to present their idea, be guided, be evaluated, and share their vision.
  - Vote on how a pool of money can be spent on the best ideas.
  - Hear reports from each presenter from prior years that have received money on what went right and what went wrong.
  - Broadcast the entire program globally, with opportunities for all presenters to receive crowd-funding, with 3% of the funding money going to the non-profit to cover expenses around the summit.
  - Provide opportunities to network and synergize and learn for all participants.
  - Have a really good time by hosting the event in countries that need income and helping them learn to host amazing events with top food, massage, and natural experiences, so that what we leave after an event is:
    - Locals with a few hundred thousand of strong currency.
    - 100 people with better service skills.
    - An infrastructure that can host other events.

- A few million people around the world are aware of the facilities and want to go there to perhaps host an event or take a vacation.

10 X Media: $1.5 million

- Invest $1.5 million in creating the 10 X Media App as outlined here: https://www.youtube.com/watch?v=1H7Ei8BXVlg
- Promote it for a 7% cut of gross media sales on the platform to anyone wishing to build a community.
- Put 50% of all income into generating and translating the most meaningful audio and videos for the platform, paying particular interest to meaningful art and books being put into audio for the first time so that more people can listen to great books while walking/working/driving.

Form a 10 X Country: $50 million:

- Buy up scrap cruise ships from the cruise industry.
- Buy scrap oil rigs.
- Position a network of vehicles in the great garbage dump in the Pacific.
- Develop the ability to recycle plastic at sea and transform it into a giant grid of flotation devices.
- Develop a business exporting flotation devices mined from the ocean to those wishing to expand the country.
- Model and test out a 10 X Country for three years in a reality TV show that paid $120 million to bring the event to the world and fund $70 million for the next iteration of a 10 X Country.

Plant 1 Billion Trees: $100 million

- Make donating $1 for 1 tree a 1 click button with reminders on our app.
- Create badges in the app and awards, including the "carbon neutral" award for planting 1,000 trees as an individual.
- Make that badge something companies can use to show their commitment to ecology.
- Educate people on the many amazing things a tree does:
    - Stops topsoil erosion.
    - Creates organic matter in the soil.
    - Creates habitat for more than 10,000 life forms.
    - Slows down temperature volatility, thus reducing wind speeds.
    - Makes it cooler in the sun and warmer at night beneath the tree.
    - Creates visual beauty.
    - Provides possible resources, including fruits.
    - Reduces dust in the air.
    - Generates cleaner air for all mammals to breathe.
    - Captures water from the soil and evaporates it from leaves, creating clouds.
- .
- Create a questionnaire that helps people learn how many trees are cut and used for their lifestyle, so they know how many trees their lifetime cut down.
- Find a depression in a barren desert within five miles of the ocean that is below sea-level and build a 5 mile tunnel to the ocean so that a few billion gallons can come in and some of that water evaporates and creates rain: $50 million
- Build a solar power desalination plant in the desert and plant all around the ocean: $30 million
- Plant 15 million trees where needed.

1000 New Cultures: $70 million

- Create an app as outlined on https://www.10xliving.org/the-app $750,000.
- Buy a 20 acre piece of land for $2 million
- Use a community center and micro-personal space design to construct $20,000. personal spaces: $1.7 million initially and subsequently funded by occupants.
- Build a 100 person community and iterate it until everyone in the community considers their lives ten times better than they were prior to joining.
- Create a reality media project to advertise the project and its impact.
- Train people in the community to be teachers and guides to license the app to other communities for $750,000 and start 12-150 person communities around the world.
- Track the impact of each culture on all stake-holders over five years.
- Fund a movie about the project: $2 million.
- Develop cultural technologies and best practices that insure peace and grace on Mars and the Moon to avoid costly conflicts.
- Create a $50 million bank to provide up to five years of funding per community for those following proven protocols.

Locating and Forming the Most Competent Team on the Planet: $15 million

- Hire three to five full time people to locate the most competent people on the planet in each of 1100 fields for three years: $1.7 million.
- Locate the most successful people in the world by results for 1000 of the most important fields.
- Invite them to create a skill assessment for their field, and to explain the basis for this skill assessment in detail, knowing that the very best people in

any field do not need money and generally love their field enough to enjoy locating others with the potential to be great in it.

- Ask each of the competent experts to nominate three peers they consider competent in their field and ask them to embellish the test for competency, explaining why each test matters.
- Open-source the tests for competency on an app.
- Translate the app into 30 languages.
- Invite the world to assess their competency for free, on condition that they are identified so they can be contacted.
- Sell this data to companies and groups who want to make money for $1,500. per search.
- Share this data with groups who are focused on global well-being.
- Create a DAO platform protocol where anyone who wants to help with certain focuses can list those focuses and anyone who wants to start a DAO can do so, and anyone who wants to get alerts when a DAO that needs their skill has been formed and can sign up.

Trauma Literacy: $50 million

- Assemble the most competent 150 people on the planet to articulate, navigate, avoid, and heal trauma.
- Give each of them $50-$150,000 to develop a course alone or as a team that includes a four hour free program for the world's population or a sub-demographic.
- Put all courses on an app for $20. suggested donation, using the 10 X Media app platform.
- Invite active critical feedback from all demographics.
- Take the 20% that have the most impact and elevate these by translating them into thirty languages.

- Give all authors the chance to refine their work for $30-100,000 if they engage with their audiences.
- Host free workshops via Zoom for teachers and students around the world who are interested: $100,000 per year per trainer/teacher/author who wants to work seven hours a day or more on this topic.
- Do comparative studies on the impact of the courses on schools that take the course and those that do not over a 12 month period.
- Seek to raise government money to expand this program to $250 million, as results validate it.

Create a DAO Protocol to Delegate these Ideas: $15 million

- Create a DAO protocol for each of these ideas, defining job-descriptions that renew every three weeks:
  - Describe the competencies needed for each role
  - Measure the competency levels of those interested in the role: 65% weight.
  - Measure peer interest in collaboration: 15% weight.
  - Measure who will do it for the least compensation: 20%
  - Whoever scores highest in this system gets the job, by agreeing to do the detailed job description.
  - Once someone has the job, they are then measured by how well they do the job description:
    - What % of the job description do they do each 3 weeks? 50%
    - Do those observing them approve: 30%
    - Are they trending up, holding steady, or trending down in becoming more and more competent: 20%
    - Is there a viable candidate who will take on the role if given to them as an alternative?

- This determines who has each role every three weeks.
- After earning three renewals they can renew every 3 months to 3 years and can put forth their reasoning for the time-period they are requesting.
- Create supporting roles for each of the main roles.
- Build an app module that fits in with the 10 X App and continues to iterate itself: $5 million
- Pay salaries defined in the DAO to delegate each of these ideas to the team most capable of implementing it: $7 million
- Pay for expenses related to these projects: $3 million.
- Use the app data to locate the most competent people on the planet to invite them to apply to the DAO's.

The Intelligence X Prize: $150 million

- Challenge anyone in the world to demonstrate their intelligence by creating the highest amount of sustainable well-being for as many people as possible per unit of money, time, and natural resources.
- Establish a standardized method of measuring well-being.
- Create a DAO of seven voluntary judges with the authority to give away: $100,000 per year
    - Give $100,000 in seed money to test ideas.
    - Grant prizes of between $10,000 and $10 million for demonstrations of intelligence that have been tested.
    - Give more priority to ideas that create enough value to be self-funding at some point.
- Create a media channel to discuss all the applications that do and don't make it and why.

- Invite direct audience participation to crowd-fund ideas on their own or pay people not officially selected.
- Invite people to donate to support the prizes.
- Invest $50 million in moderately secure loans for projects that support the planet's well-being in various ways and in for-profit technologies that have a reasonable chance of appreciating in value so that this fund does not run out.

Universal Basic Income: $150 million

- Locate the top five most vulnerable populations on the planet, measured by access to food, medicine, and basic shelter.
- Prioritize 100,000 people out of this demographic in a particular region for the purpose of tracking well-being and all impacts over a ten year period.
- Create a list from the population and experts outlining the structural shifts that would help them become sustainable in shelter and food: $1 million
- Provide $5 million or more in material costs for them to improve their infrastructure.
- Provide food, shelter, and education for anyone willing to work six hours or more improving their town/city/community.
- Create a reality media show outlining progress, challenges, and more in which the audience can donate time, money, and natural resources: $150,000.
- Invest $10 million in an investment account in Crypto and Tesla that people are able to sell 30% of the amount the fund appreciates to provide basic income for the care of people who cannot work due to age or disability.
- Assess overall happiness after 5 years.

Free Education for Humanity: $100 million

- Invite citizens of each country via public television and YouTube to submit the texts and training sources that have brought the most well-being to their lives.
- Nominate the top 150 sources from every country, where they differ.
- Buy the rights to freely share these texts with the world.
- Translate the texts and media into 30 languages.
- Make this freely available and updated to everyone in the world in audio, written, and video format, inviting discussion and participation with the 10 X Media app.

The Global Psychedelic Institute: $7.5 million

- Select a global location hospitable to psychedelic use for medical and evolutionary purposes.
- Create optimum settings for profoundly meaningful experiences.
- Equip these settings with unobtrusive instruments to gather meta-data about every experience.
- Develop psychedelic protocols and test them on healthy volunteers to determine the best results.
- Publish the meta-data in real-time online.
- Create a place online where anyone can share anecdotal data.
- Invite scientists, sociologists, and people interested in human potential to lead and explore frontiers of consciousness in which all things are recorded.

The Intelligence Media Network: $72 million

- Do a global survey on the media that generates the most sustainable well-being:

- Take 11,000 pieces of timeless media of all types, including dance, music, and the like.
- Establish a rating system that measures how much well-being comes from engaging per piece of media per person.
- License the right to publish this media for public education: $10 million.
- Set up a portal protocol with DAO's and a feedback loop so that submitting media, bidding for it, getting feedback, and selecting it is automatic.
- Create three channels per region/language 24/7 that distribute and invite local engagement with the media:
    - Questions and answers with authors.
    - Action steps and measuring impact on local groups.
    - Audience stories and interviews.
    - Ideas nominated and crowd-funded.
    - A $50 million bank to provide $10 million seed capital for 3 regions to demonstrate the ideas that can come from public crowd-funding and that the public can have way more fun creating local media they like and funding it than relying on large film studios. This could include giving $100k budgets to high schools around the world and more to the schools that create the best media and can become self-funding by people willing to buy the media.

The Better Idea Fund: $100 million

- There will be unexpected costs related to the ideas above.
- There will be better ideas than the above ideas that emerge in the process of pursuing them.
- There will be expedient opportunities to have massive positive impact that require capital.

- For all of these reasons almost 20% of the budget is reserved for these possibilities.
- It will be invested until used:
    - In Tesla 30%
    - In Ether 35% and Bitcoin 15%
    - In secured loans to non-profits and individuals at 5% interest 20%

It should be noted that in 11 years it is highly likely that the fund and its assets would be valued at $500 million - $3 billion due to appreciating investments, and the fact that many of these projects have high commercial value. The goal over time is to do all of these things and generate a 50% return on capital, such that there is money to do even more.

What is your answer to the question: "What is the most intelligent way to transform $1 billion into sustainable well-being for yourself and others?

ABOUT THE AUTHOR

At an early age, I discovered the difference between normal and intelligent. It turns out that the majority is never up to date with the latest technology in either thought, well-being, or engineering. A tremendous amount of cruelty, waste, and stupidity is the result of not re-examining the status quo in all arenas. This led me to prioritize intelligent design as the most potent skill in answer to the question: "What skill, if learned well, could be most useful to humanity over the next one hundred years?"

First as a landscape designer, then as a site-developer, and then as an author of books and protocols for conscious relationships, design has been a theme. As a sensitive, I am conflict averse and default to a much more private and low-profile life. The experience of extreme cruelty, abuse of power, and trauma led to a desire to engage more actively in the creation of a more intelligent culture, which resulted in forming several non-profits. I've always learned by speaking, writing, and teaching what I want to get better at, so this book began as a lighthouse to help guide my own non-profit efforts. Now that I know what I want to do with my life, it just takes a bit of postage and extra effort to share these ideas with you, in the hope they support your own vision.

If you would like to share how these ideas have helped you clarify your mission please write to me at: dane@happinessdata.org

Made in the USA
Columbia, SC
28 September 2024